Holler

Other books by Alice Burdick

Voice of Interpreter (The Eternal Network, 1993)
Fun Venue (The Eternal Network, 1994)
Signs Like This (The Eternal Network, 1994)
Covered (Letters, 1994)
Simple Master (Pedlar Press, 2002)
The Human About Us (BookThug, 2002)
Flutter (Mansfield Press, 2008)

Holler

Alice Burdick

Mansfield Press

a stUart ross book

Copyright © Alice Burdick 2012
All rights reserved
Printed in Canada

Library and Archives Canada Cataloguing in Publication

Burdick, Alice
Holler / Alice Burdick.

Poems.
ISBN 978-1-894469-70-8

I. Title.

PS8553.U6267H65 2012   C811'.54   C2012-900846-X

Editor for the press: Stuart Ross
Typesetting & cover design: Stuart Ross
Cover image: *Geisha*, Dana Holst, 2006
Author photo: Nancy McCarthy

The publication of *Holler* has been generously supported by
the Canada Council for the Arts and the Ontario Arts Council.

Canada Council for the Arts   Conseil des Arts du Canada   ONTARIO ARTS COUNCIL   CONSEIL DES ARTS DE L'ONTARIO

Mansfield Press Inc.
25 Mansfield Avenue, Toronto, Ontario, Canada M6J 2A9
Publisher: Denis De Klerck
www.mansfieldpress.net

This one goes out to all the humans.

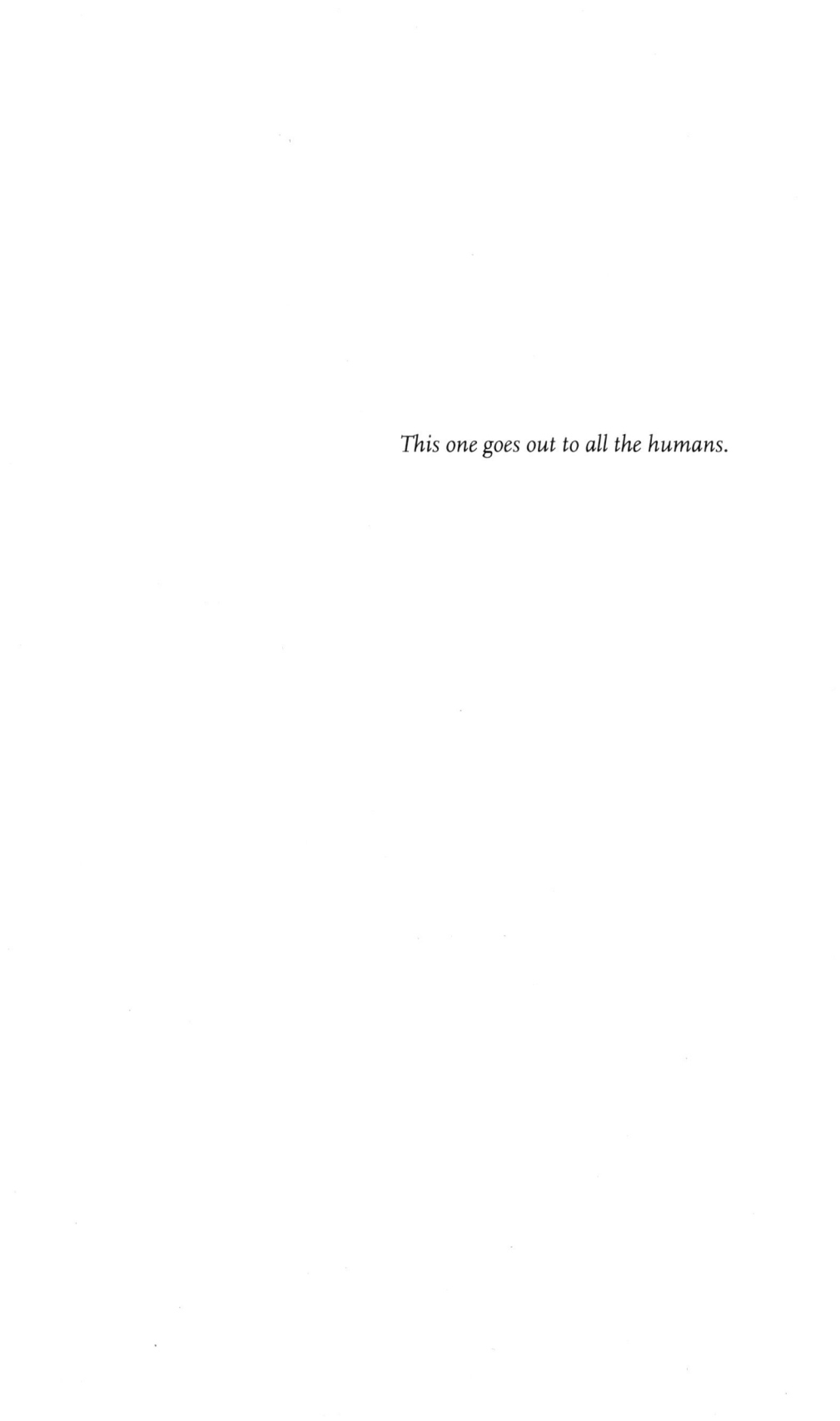

Contents

Nothing fancy / 9
Rats, chipmunks, whatever / 10
Another book? Another book? / 11
Black box / 12
Ham raffle / 14
Holler / 15
Fall idyll / 16
Who knows the knees / 17
Mahone Bay rhapsody / 18
Voices of the familiar / 21
Ghost feet / 22
Rain dream / 23
No regret / 24
Absence makes the heart / 25
Banal / 26
The wonder / 27
Youth camp / 28
Baby wheels / 29
Motes / 30
On the teeth / 31
Sword brain / 32
Flood zoo / 33
Life from jeopardy / 34
Scenic route / 35
Champion sleep / 36
Age fugue / 37
Attractive and efficient / 38
Toddler moan / 39
Big move / 40
So so spirit / 41
Voices / 42
Thanks / 43
Silent plan / 44

Brains heart zombies / 45
Big sound / 46
Broken in our field / 47
Earl / 48
Flesh mob / 49
Tryptich for Ed / 50
Generational / 52
Snow / 53
Winter repair / 54
Cottage party, buckets / 55
Girl stuff / 56
Steerage / 57
Soft garments / 58
Winter bug / 60
Brown robes / 61
Nor'easter / 62
The layers / 63
What happened / 64
Generous to a fart / 65
Snow drops / 66
The wandering sandbar / 67
Know thine enema / 68
Policy / 69
How magical! / 70
All the same / 72
Pro orgone / 73
Daylight's party / 74
Remembrance Day, 2011 / 75
Body House / 76

Nothing fancy

The sparkling lights of nothing,
honey. Nothing fancy,
nothing empty, always full
of sand. Hands through grains
of former humans, petrified logs
submerged in water. Remember the forest
as the trees yawn into bright fire.
Compressed grains of bile and treasure,
a cake if you will of creation.
Simpering birds on the veranda,
aiming for the desired field-guide photos.
I want to be a special bird.
What does the moon mean?
Where does the air fly
when it's all breathed out?

Rats, chipmunks, whatever

Hello, human, do you like faces?
Return to the floor
and drool all you want.
Laugh at the new day
because it's pretty funny.
The open sun drops
a splash onto the red toy.
Arthur smiles when I tickle his chins.
Plastic tree over plastic elephant;
the plastic folk recline,
hair immobile, heads spinning,
abandoned in the empty pot.

Another book? Another book?

Once upon a time, next week,
I will light a fire on the stairs.
Three wolves in total will sleep
on or near the fridge. A piece of apple
will enlarge three times
due to cat hair and lint.
The blue jays will find a way
to balance on the windowpanes.
All the books in this house will
become human
and tear themselves apart, so what.

What should I feed the wolves
to keep them all at bay?

Black box

Flippant despair,
skinny people trying to lose weight.
First-world superheathens afraid of toxins:
what I say is not what I do.
I am a banana in such a specific time zone.

I make a heart turn green and fall out into the cosmos.
It took 3 million years to look this way, shrivelled up
blackened rock. Black box of history and denial.

Squeaks from the further room,
sounding like an accordion complex.
I wish I sounded more like Harpo's instrument,
foot up on a crooked elbow, suddenly schmaltzy
but appropriate for the long-gown crowd.

People compare notes on beatitude
through breastfeeding. It's just something
you do, not an awards show! A halo
won't appear each time you let your kid
eat a knife or pee onto your leg, sorry.

Just the multiple stains of life.
Imagine me, without a larynx,
my greatest fear: no eyes,
no oven. No cooking implements
but no tears from sliced onions.

Mists of time revolt
us. We people stop being pretty
and sink into our addictions,
become fat or thin,
drunk or absent,
or all of this together.

Bird me a tree,
bird me a stick on the ground,
no sleep for insects,
eyes yawned into the breech.
Dogs, dogs, dogs
stop passersby at the playground.
Ignoring the children
for cute obedient puppies.

Ham raffle

Order me some
hams and bacons,
because I want to win the big one.

The conversation officer
idles his truck at the four-way,
letting off smoke
and mirrors.

Holler

Despair is for the living,
so we're very much a hive
of proven hope and then a dive
into the breath of misery.

People yell the authentic.
It means a horse, its speed,
its truck into the median;
its hoarse indictment of our incessant greed.

Trickle treat,
we self-made prostitutes,
so very fond of
our invisible thighs.

Fall idyll

Woodpecker hammers at the corner of our house.
Zane says let her go at it,
there are bugs in there.
I feed the baby and the child,
and the house feeds the bugs and the birds.

Compost grows and sinks,
darkens and heats,
sunflower already mainly
pecked away before the winter.

What I have is all around me.
A man who loves and works hard,
two children who play and love hard,
and friends who make the other spheres ring.

Outside the window,
Hazel trails Zane through the yard,
picking up kale and rocks
as Arthur points at things we don't fully see.
The crack in the window is lengthening
to let in the October mist.

Some ducks just stick around,
dawdle on the Maggie Maggie
and the banks near the Saveasy,
maybe look above at others flying south,
chomping on some dissolving buns.

Who knows the knees

Letting the grey in,
letting it out itself, just
as clouds do, we know what they're like,
hairy and floating about up there. Something rises,
steam or some other breath. Bouncing around
in a not exactly rhythmic way, the body shouts,
especially the knees. Who knows the knees
knows the needs of the joints we all know.

Mahone Bay rhapsody

Stern discussions of possible weights.
Glossy stains on the older older floors.
Air that moves faster than the machinery fails.
The friendly faces in translation, long-term blank-out,
please tickle my neck. Things on lawns, trees exploding
from a metal round. How to determine the speed
of demolition? Pasta dries at its own rate,
just flour and water. Teeth like noodles
scattered on the floor. Fling the air onto the water.
A star on the firmament. Lake of speeds, torsion
of blinking torsos. Wax and red tables.
Ceramic eyes and ears. Noses that smell the hope
exhaled from glass doors. Wooden salvage roads,
the routes into the news, the waves,
the waves of cold water.

What do you do? When do you stop?
How long would you go to retrieve a body,
a human you know, declared missing, meaning maybe
a misstep, a piece of ice broken and afloat?
Even a small place that hooks onto the edge of the continent
like that rusty fish catcher.

Actual child voices! Out in the streets!
Raised above the gracious murmurs of the genteel
boiled wool crowd. I'd so like to connect,
whatever the age, but often the looks veer towards
distaste, disdain, a tough look to receive when convincing
a small child not to wail like a kettle on boil.

Delicious occasional outings, walking
at the speeds to which I was once accustomed.
Thinking of space and words, no caution.

How to disturb the melting snow. Tender
patient soil waits for months on end. Barely present,
if possible, in mixed-use spaces. I owe you,
I owe me, a hot bobbing past.

Cars fill up on gas, and let gas out into the air,
floating above the bay. Mound of snow hides,
like a government information blackout. Do not
even think about what lies below the crusting snow.
Both crawling vehicles and those that speed
won't stop at crosswalks for crossing families.

A framed opening into the familiar symbols and signals
of the town. Who are "they"? The entire community
and the singular entities. The big metal thing stopped
next to the plank of concrete, and the waterflesh creatures
scramble out and skip up the wooden boards, through
glass, metal, plaster, and a whole plot's worth of wood.
We can all say we live in the woods still. Decimated
and reassembled, no sap, but woods still, made singular.

What are the cells saying? We wonder how we breathe.
The nose stops working if there's too much self-reflection.
Space changes overall. Round empty red-beaded pupil.
Rockabilly in an empty room. Black, almost Amish balance
of wood and colour. High contrast with the ornate gingerbread

that eats this town. A walk down the pretty streets, watching
the cannibalistic fairy-tale tricksters in conservative
outerwear mowing, primping, tidying.

Do you understand the wonder of conversation?
I enjoy the sound of a couple talking, their venture
a possible stomach ache, but a venture even so.
Howl at the wind, trick it into a calm breeze.
The ducks too live here all year.
They swim in the water and walk on the ice.

Voices of the familiar

Low pressure in an elevated state.
Curing sausages with disease of circumlocution.
Heart swell or muscle spasm at the cold light
of skin in the morning. A small body or two
fitting into my side. Plastic locusts stream
onto the silt and water. Voices of the familiar.

A man who hops and dances, waiting at corners,
later wheeled down Maple by a slow complainer
and her dog on squat legs. Boredom of repetitive
family strain disorder. I need a new glimpse
at the old ennui and stubborn fate.

Day sifts through light branches.
Bug slapped, bug down, bug down.
Sounds of machines in the leaves.
Orderly workers on sound houses.
Money lost and never had, paper paper,
bouncing charts. Blood pools in toes,
bruise moving over the top of my foot.
Musical notes, sings Hazel,
and Arthur says water
when he sees ducks.

Ghost feet

Please make me a book
from salad and tears. I cry at condiments.
My ghost feet light up the sidewalk.
Will you forget a book or a person so easily?

Arthur makes a series of sounds
that will one day be words.
He gets his point across
the floor, straight to the cat's dish.

Rain dream

The nap you claim
makes you wake into light-
filled water, floating
into the open source
of young memory,
mainly composed
of new understanding.

Cats don't land on their feet
all the time, but the odds
are that's where they look at you, eyes wide,
purring, eating things they shouldn't.

Grass slurps into the overbrush.
Outside there is rain.
Inside, rain.
I am rain and you are rain.
We are a bunch of fun gumboots.

Flee the raft! It doesn't even
match the understory.
Something about a match
in a haystack, or a needle in a fire.
Anyway, I am never up to date
with the anti-venom. But who is?

No regret

Oh yes, I meant to say goodbye.
But there was no time. There is never
no time, or always a small slice
of time, in which to grow horns
and fangs. Leap out into the past,
arms open in a kite way, breathing
storm clouds and false hopes.

Absence makes the heart

It must be telepathy,
branches of thought spindled into clouds.
Up there, there are brains
that look like clouds,
whispering clues of their absence.

Absence makes the heart.
Grow bolder in the streaking mystery—
the lake doesn't explain itself.
Leeches decide to attach
to flesh of all ages, why not,
it all contains veins of blood,
pulsing pulsing through capillary waves.

Fix the elliptical
so it tilts into comprehension.
Hush, for the birds won't screech
so. Tilt so the stairs won't creak so.

Banal

I see the shadow of the squash,
comfy on the tablecloth.
Vegetables round out the day
of toys and vehicles. Eat a piece
of historical romance, the steam
from compost swarms the owls.

Please, please, don't be loud.
Don't retrieve the losing way.
Let it go, and let speech come.
It's impossible to win an argument
with a three-year-old. She will
wear you down with steady shrieks
and logic that comes and goes.
Waves of understanding
and intent.

The wonder

Wind moves over,
garden doors removed,
small bushes lean
into the larger.

Wind's slow shriek,
but indoors it's much louder,
a higher pitch, and calm again.
"You want to come up!"
Makes an ululation slow
into a comment on a rowboat.

Ball, hey, momma.
Feed me a stream of interest,
a playmate to the hard floor.

Things go walking by.
What are they? Are they round
or human or
do they belong to the cookie store?

My nose is here,
on my face. Your arms are there,
on your body. We swing
all together, and put on sweaters
to go outside. Still,
we wonder at the chewed-up papers,
the broken toys.

Youth camp

Hear me, hear me,
give me more,
don't say more.

I want you to hug me.
I want food.
Where does that go?

I don't want to do that anymore.
I'm fine for now.
It's a little bit wet here, on the floor.

Baby wheels

Wheel into brake, moisture
content inexplicably gathering
on the surfaces of home.
Faces into the birth pool,
singular gasping, attempts
to understand the code words.
Blessed or blessing,
blessing be, some frequent curse
of constraint and flowered eyes.

What's happened to you, baby?
You used to be entirely air,
and now you're arrow,
part imbedded in a tree.

The growling group of human
family enters the house,
up and down the octaves,
breathing life and sticky handprints.

Motes

Yes, things go walking by,
or they fly, even better,
they swim through air
as Hazel describes,
hands moving out,
little airplanes.

My gut, my back,
attached I hear
some belt of despair,
strange pangs of muscular entropy.

Come along,
enter the picture,
but beware: everyone
there is dead. They see you
but don't exist,
just like memory.

Clues show up,
no warning as usual,
but they lead me into stories
I did not write.

I smell pumpkin.
It smells strong.
It is leaves rotting
into the lawn.

On the teeth

On the teeth,
an arrow, in the heart
a pulsing bag of blood.
In the arms, some skin
stretched tight or bagging
slightly with the years,
ears sinking lower
on the bulb of skull.
Tongue longer, longing
for lost words.

Sword brain

Dance with me,
indulgent creatures,
spinning on bums
or waving arms around your ears.

I have nipples.
That and the belly button
mean I came from people
and can give like a person,
despite all the evidence otherwise.
At least I have this generic proof.

Stuck mollusk-like
to the base of a ship of drooling
fools. Holding on, eyes closed,
basic antennae reach to the other shells.
Are you there? Have you ever been?

Digestion in the house of boxes
and tunnels, roundabout into repeated
dreams and echoes. Instant correction
to be depended on, defense
of the sword brain.

Sword brain,
dance with me,
indulgent creature
with your unerring grace
a note of sweet finality.

Flood zoo

Llamas huddle in a manger,
gibbons piss and play. Toys
from daycare, familiar plastic,
hurled around the breathe-through cage.

One wedge of air,
the clouds, the clouds!
And black or purple sweeps the sky,
an eyelid over the rolling land,
rivers near the tropical birds.
Wild fat cats' eyes change irises
to view new afternoon night,
and the ponies lower their lashes
in the small walkable pens.

A puddle keeps on filling,
so there's no way but through,
a total submergence into the weather.
It pools and comforts our wet origins.
It mirrors our hesitant frogginess.

Life from jeopardy

Sitting around,
learning life from jeopardy.
Is it real?
No problem.
Check out the frost,
water on the floor,
each boot on the wrong foot.

Turtles crawl over the pillow,
all in the same direction,
hiccing-up into the air
and flying to the shorn island.

Scenic route

I won't buy the round device
that restrains children
in the water. All I see are trucks,
trucks and ducks. Ducks
on the shore, gaining on the tourist
throwing bread. Eagle flies
so close to our car, straight across the highway,
its totally feathered body waves,
its eyes in fact are totally round.

Champion sleeper

Each day it's so gravity,
hip bones slip apart and the spine
declines to remain upright.

Kick sand into the dream.
The doors are open for charity purposes.
Residents will feel a dangerous breeze,
a gathering source of progeny.

Eyes open into a dark and vein-lit pod.
Does the squid see our dreams
and graph the present from these?
Jars of water over years
become more air, after all.
You can't defy water and air—
they ignore disdain.

Monstrous seizures in boardrooms
on the 34th floor. We should send
a letter from our cave in the mouth
of a compliant duck.

Shadow of a serrated edge on the guava can.
Twins of spruce look out for the birch
that fall to the scythe each June.
Everything is an import.

Drool will make me the champion sleeper,
traitor to beauty, folds everywhere.

Age fugue

Just because I'm weird
doesn't mean I'm wrong.
Put that in your heart and smoke it.

I walk through the clouds
over the post office, heave off
the mist everywhere, socks drooping
as usual, but not necessary
because I'm flying.

Is the theme of this year offence?
Why is each slight deflected
into hurt feelings? Victorian miasma
of don't say that. Forty must mean
I call bullshit every damn day.

Flammable eyes,
built-in dehydrators.
Mystical antecedents with the names
mom and pop, peeking out through
smoked-up antique-store glass.

Why make me be?
How did that happen?
It's a glorious road with no stop signs,
but many crosswalks that must be obeyed.
Please, just look and wait
so it doesn't feel like you want to kill
my family and me.

At some point,
perhaps yesterday,
or when I'm 80, I'll know the reason
for all these stinking time bombs.

Attractive and efficient

My nose smells
the glorious death
going on in the garden.
Life folds over into its collection
box a root, a hand, a limb, a leaf—
make composition fall
into a seasonal charade.

Tomatoes are waiting,
the vines are falling down.
Neighbours look down noses
at our demented lawn,
where mice build tunnels
against the gathering chill.

Toddler moan

Down near the water,
a sliced-open teddy bear:
who did you hear
crying up there?

Nope, nope, nope.
Each square fits into a bright green cup,
a box into a box,
an animal at rest,
totally yellow.

A fork into circumstance:
where were you at 3 a.m.?

Blessing the fractures.
Blessing the spiders
mending the fractures.

Big move

Soon to banish the previous house
and on to the town, where the child's arms
and legs and hair will grow out
through small windows.

Moving to the past
or future, whatever you want
to call it, where water sits
and light clings to water, eyeballs slither
into their nests and dream
what they once saw.

My callow bones sing out
hollow occasions,
the doctors hit by large head
injuries or claims of big associations.

So so spirit

Exteriors are endlessly replaced,
and the core carries on.
Don't know where I am,
gauze draped over a mysterious
shoulder, eyes dropped
into an earth hole.

Atoll of memory,
silent background water,
a splash into the past,
as it carries life away.

Rapping is so Victorian,
tables moving on ectoplasmic
cones, a voice in tenor.
Presence a performance;
a sweet odour emitting
from the newfangled phone.

Who are you?
I can't remember,
shredded as I was
when the lights went out.

Voices

The phone is full
of hot air, a bellows.
But it's not ghosts,
no, don't worry—
air is just a huge sound
in a small space.

What you think are voices
are voices, yes, but your
own brain has made them,
a many-chambered thing,
full of words known since "go."
So open up your mouth
and let them out into the hot air
of the receiver, so the other
ear can hear 'em.

All sounds the sound.
Peel back the outside
and make it inner.
Heartbeat steady crash.

Thanks

The ball! The ball!
Arthur slides along the floor,
trained cobra, eyes on the ball,
which is a squash,
sphere enough for bouncing.
Cloth over his shoulders,
talking back to books.

Let's go for a little walk,
spend the time that is moist
out on the mossing sidewalks,
speed in an up and down way
through the lives of worms and leaves.

Well, hello, potty,
you fine and useful receptacle.
Let's talk shit.
Every day, void your contents,
retaining what is useful. Don't be shy
about the vitamins and minerals—
they have no shame. Energy
sure likes its journey through our passages.
And that's the story of food.

Overwrought delivery—
not that we get that here.
We veto handheld foodstuffs.
But mercy, a speech into a pillow,
so loud to the dust mites.

Silent plan

Ninja priests slide
into rooms, so quiet,
must be the training.

Silent saving, praying
into open mouths
where the air went out.

Brains heart zombies

We think only what our brains allow—
our zombies are in control.
Slip once and they scatter, afraid of the fire
of happenstance. Righted, they lurch
their way through the repetitive day.
And we are proud of ourselves,
though we hardly know what we're made of,
from where our impulses reach and grasp
and hang our brainpan hats.

I taste cherries. I taste bees.
They rode on the cherries into my mouth,
which opened to receive them, due to the zombies,
who love a parade of venom, stingers, and fuzz.

All the mystery is inside here,
in our dark and hardhat heads.

Big sound

From silence a big sound
of doors and dogs and wind
comes in. Former stance
on stairs and rugs,
huddled under sounds.

Sometimes silence
scares us, for the big
noise it produces.

Leather air
through the shoe-store door.

Broken in our field

Eddy is a woman cat.
No, he is a man cat.
Is he a man cat, mommy?

The news from afar
is just like the news from right here.
Reptiles are much more impressive when they move into the dark.
The light makes us awkward.
We hold our hair up with fingers
and try to exfoliate scales;
no use, they're part of us.
Rust gathers as frost does.
Trees chopped down
take the axes with them,
and bury them in the forest.
I heard it. I heard the trees.
The leaves parted and the moon jumped
over the field of tipping cows.

Ash tree,
you bird magnet,
standing broken in our field.

Earl

Swimming air in,
finally, cool breath.
Connect! says Hazel,
and Arthur scoots to wheels.

Flesh mob

Flesh mob.
Rubble rabble,
distant squawk on the ear
plane, closer hover further
crash. Pleased to meet
your maker. It is a matter
of muttering space lights,
a trade at the bandstand at dusk.
Give me your old bulbs
and I'll hand you a lead.
Your dogs are truly four-legged
and nose specific. Please
give them a nice low divan
or scoop of something warm in plastic.

Triptych for Ed

1

Ed moves lightly over the floors,
from the kitchen, circle, to the living room,
circle, in a circle through the house,
the only sound of him
his unretracted claws,
clicking his neurological route.

Injection of water
into a cat who nears 21,
but won't make it.
His body is interested,
but his brain is looking
to the other world.

A present memory
sitting on my shoulder,
a purring kitten in the old cheese store.

2

As usual—
or is it later?—
I speak too soon.
The cat awaits his rose-hip cake,
marker of his 21st year.
What keeps him on?
His legs and paws, the water
in a cup, the moist chunks
he gnaws, such a big fan of gravy.

Rain in the new year,
snowman slowly recedes,
carrot drops to the ground.
The snow butt is more pronounced
as blue jays fly by, heads cocked
to wonder, is this structure food?

3

Exactly one week later.
One week ago, that small grey cat
was propped on my pillow.

The coldest day of the winter yet,
wind blowing, brilliant blue sky.
Fir boughs place where Ed's small body lies,
deeper and colder than his entire life.

One step into the ground,
and another through the stars.

Generational

There is a ghost in the air,
just hanging there, exacting sound
like a blade. When you have no mouth,
you use what's at hand. Air to water, water to steam,
dreams shining through the windows and lighting
the night in pieces. How many moons
can you count, ghost? How many invisible
stars are embedded in the bird dreams?

The marginal id makes its presence known
with the shadows stretching over trees
and mounds of snow. Heat pours out
from eyes and ears, a roar of fear,
circle of sadness and memory.

Downstairs the kids keep
the conversation up with the elders,
climbing on the furniture
and throwing cars around.

Snow

Every tree
a birch
in winter.

Winter repair

Sawing walls in winter,
holing up and flapping curtains.
You place the machine on the wall, the machine
that sucks bad humours out into the running stream
of existential air. Huh? Who's there?

My funny valentine,
like the pain of the slight-slipped elbow,
or some long ode to a heart
or at least all of its ways in and out.

A constant sawing, shreds
of wall on the counter, sure
I like a cup of new air or dammed ice
just like all the rest of us.

And fleas? No other animals
but these extremely small biting bouncers,
climbing and leaping great distances
to fill with blood.

It's not enough to carve a hole;
you've got to take your sweater off
and freeze the end of your nose.
Go ahead and turn off the heat in February.

Cottage party, buckets

Friendly friends,
smoking wheelbarrows as snow
scurries through the thinned birches.

Some water is flowing somewhere.
It's made of small stones
and wind worn by the air.
I take a glass of it and you want to drink it,
so it is now all yours.

Early spring ice floe—
Molega made it float
a lengthwise sliver
over the hardtack waves.

Whole pepitas
pop out two full days later.

Girl stuff

Mashed-open heart,
mâché in a box,
hole in the middle,
a fine base to impale.

Is this styrofoam a ring, mommy?
It is, Hazel, it is.
What do I want, mommy?
You must tell *me* that.

The story of pink as one colour only
in a thick book of colours. Unicorns
were frequently fierce,
their horns holy impalers.
Rhinos without glitter
would be great on little t-shirts.

Cornered by princesses,
the girl cowers in the corner
till she grabs her own unicorn
and scares the regal gremlins away.

Steerage

Steerage won't accept me.
The wheels are way too big.
If I reach up, the windows are too high,
they are always open,
and the wind keeps coming in.

Soft garments

All we remember is the grey sweep of sky, not falling down on us, but all around as we float. Day is an idea of the animals who'd prefer water without fluoride, twigs in a circle, language centred on the rocks. I form an 'a' and it becomes the look of a steer's head, language in reverse. All the walls climb with flowers. Each room a different hothouse. Somebody really scored big at the discount wallpaper centre.

When you feel a body near you, but you do not see the body, it is just a low-level electrical buzz. That's how elves see it, and the ghosts think we're made of protein powder, coagulated forms that don't stop moving until we are there in the grey sweep.

Each day there's a reminder of the people who swept the stairs, who ate eggs Benny in diners, who wrapped us in soft garments, winter boots, hilarious makeup. Strange how the lobes recall stories that otherwise wish to disappear. Do you remember the outlets? The wash of warm weather in the distant pool, a few other tourists swimming vacant? The tall green leaves, the vines that wrapped themselves around extinguished walls? Each ruined house held many. Each person who passed through left something behind. A coin, a breath, a muttered curse, and, every now and then, a life.

Would you make that sound grow dimmer in a pillow? A little fox and the little fox's house, a bubble in a hand, sphere on its way through fingers. The mother fox and her kits housing in a hole in the demolished old motel grounds on the outskirts of town. Not to be continued, though, as the condos soon rose up.

We are so surprised by nature. Animals walk up to us on trails and are curious. We are alarmed as we haven't seen them in a while; we've forgotten them outside of our garish kids' books and cartoons. An animal tells a joke but we don't laugh because we're afraid of other languages. My home is so structured as your home moves and moves, pushed out as trees are chopped.

Empty lot of crows and cats. The occasional dog leaps out behind bushes. Humans regularly get walked in all directions, plastic bags in lariats everywhere. Get their furry friends in to be photographed by depressive Santa, his wig askew and Shih Tzu.

Winter bug

Ladybug hits the light
at 8:03 p.m.
A tap on plastic-covered
window, closed,
another eye blinks open.

Brown robes

Mendicant friars shift logs
in the fireplace, dust and smells,
incense and sloughed cells,
rise from their various robes.

Slices of dusty light
alight on the stones that make the house
cold but solid. I wonder if each monk
has a face, or just a space
where he used to be.

Rhapsodies in the mass howl,
divination on the hills
of beans, a range of silver
pieces and water over all.

What is it with all these wet socks
and halos?

Nor'easter

Will the roof stay whole?
Why are they part horses, mommy?
They fly all over the glen.
The ocean above us,
tin roof of glass openings.
A shirt, once sweated in,
re-sweats its contents and stinks up the room.
Wind shakes
an idea of air.
Jade plant juicy,
so the cat ate it.

Glassine structures stretched
over a glorious template
all burst. We know how
to breathe our hosts in,
plants and plantations,
planets of thirst.
Sun hot as an eyeball
through a keyhole.
Pattern theory of a smoking ear.

For the first time
I strangle a fast speed.
Storming lines, balcony
of trust. All lined up,
ready to plant,
glistening radishes on the seed packets.

The layers

The words turn from voices to surfaces,
the skipping taps,
some sort of world conference
of source-touching adherents.

Out the window, the same
sifting world-sky continuum.
The sky swirls down onto the ground,
and the cold mist slips into bones
and slows a girl right down.

Another layer on
the layers over the layers.
Tea puffs out into the room
in a mouthless exhalation.

What happened

A chicken ate my heart.
Sternly, I forced angels
on the snow. Enforced my fairies
on the growing dusk.

They all leap so high,
these mystic fleas,
ordnance of teeth when you're
just a little bullet.

I gritted my teeth
because I read it in a book,
and the moon rested her big butt
down on the downy vague clouds.

Hello, gloom.
Hello, plume of nasal spray—
artificial or not, you're made of mist.

Generous to a fart

You think you don't participate in the ruling structure,
but it participates in you.
It makes you think you can avoid making choices.
It exists even stronger for your passivity.

Harpo puts his leg in your arms,
a shy and hopeful smile on his face.
Harper puts his foot in his mouth
and chews it till it's bloody.

Clean the stains from the grout
before it sets for another four years,
and we're stuck with a grim and hateful
devourer of hope.

Generous to a fart,
hot air from all the sound holes.

Sorting seeds in a soft sortie,
sun hits the roof and glances off
the trenchant observatories.

Where are you when the air falls?
Why does the world make you work
so much?

Snow drops

Snow drops
from sky to ground,
all one colour.
When light stops,
a monotone outside,
and a total removal of sound.

The wandering sandbar

I'll hollow a new song.
Speech is such a tangent to the birds,
screeching on their limbs.

Walk out through the lowered sky
as it skims our foreheads,
our buffered baffled brows,
wondering why the air breathes
its body through our noses
and back into the leaves.

The wandering sandbar
steps out of the water
and floats for the stranded
on the great salt sea.
We are big pots of water,
a tea of blood and skin,
trying our feet at walking
like flying in a dream.

A swift flies out of a chimney
and the inside of the face, a skull
transfers its frame onto the skin.
So when my mouth opens, teeth hide,
and the voice wipes the sounds gone.

Know thine enema

Each air passes through
the channels of the body,
steep corners of shifting organs.

My residue is a film at 11.
It's a story of glory and horsewhips.
Snaking trees through roots
of blood and saliva,
the imprint of our passage.

Once here,
now gone
fishing for compliments
or a reason for the intense grey.
Rain for weeks till the sidewalks
float gently on the waves.
Flowers strain to open,
taller than the utility vans
parked open-mouthed and fuming.

Policy

The man practiced his music,
opened his throat to let the toads
charm out. Oh populace,
inside those eyes, those cold blue stones,
a bucket of sand shakes out.
A subtle shift into sirocco
of lost liberty and fearsome fear.

How magical!

Lots of horns
alight on the brassiere of the goddess.
She is made of a giant fern,
I don't know how she does it,
waving frond and furling and unfurling
finite days of green.
Make this day a wise one,
or at least not too stupid.
Memory evaporates into dreams,
on its way out on life's exhalation.

Is this life, right now?
I forget because it is not taught
or learned, it's just air
and stuff, people you know,
are born from, or birth,
or just careen off of in busy streets,
or wonder at in the grocery store.

And oh, the animals! How many
with multiple textures
and desires, I bet the goddess knows
all of it. Her ears are shaped from
conch shells or maybe sinkholes,
and her mouth appears to be
a Venus flytrap, how appropriate!
Words sink in, the world sinks in,
and is swallowed to become
more words, and into the world again.

Some birds decided to hop
through the tall grass, and learn
a language that could be shared
with various predators,
especially housecats, to work
out alternatives to being devoured.
The cats learned the language,
then pretended they hadn't,
because why quit the stalk?

Oh, the pretty garlic
smells like little baby bulbils
and earthworms that like
a kick in the flavour segment.
Brylcreemed insects sing out
from the newborn plants,
one limb waving, the others clasping
so the wind doesn't take them out,
still singing, into the bay.

Hovering, or hoovering the spring
up into tiny and very sharp jaws,
humming and spat-footed.

All the same

Butter horns,
cat on the counter
leaves an impression.

I should be asleep.
Maybe, am I?
It's the end of the beginning
of the night or day,
a time when the windows
show the inside
same as outside.

Pro orgone

You are so very positive,
I can't tell you no, you should stay
and harvest your organs
or organize your rage.

I don't need you either,
Harper. You have a bad taste
in your mouth, and it shows
on your face when you spit
us right out.

If you're not busy
can you visit Mahone Bay
and shovel out my driveway?

Each law, each ear,
each shout you deny
will be kept and redoubled
so you won't return.

Just sit down and stare
at your hands and the papers
and then be gone finally
on your long vacation.

Daylight's party

Stream on, sweet sun,
illuminate the strange limbs,
fallen eyes, cold hands from
lost mittens, the sharp fuzz
of eyelids cover. Smoke of light,
golden bridge of daylight,
leaves fall on the concrete,
enormous sound of nothing.

Freaky falling leaves
show the passage of time down
along with our spines, down
into our feet, then the ground.
Ah, it's a sweet composition,
the fiesta of decomposition,
party into the basement fire
or creeping mould.

Vague counter-culture,
meaning the cups keep hitting the floor.

Remembrance Day, 2011

Hoarse declamations in the water
make bubbles. Language bubbles
back into its origins, some insensible murmur
noting the way waves feel, nothing more.
To remember on a particular day means
the pomp must be a flood of memory,
not nostalgia. Not nostalgia
for an absent past, some hologram of delusion,
hope for a changed origin, some glory.

Some glory makes the flowers wilt,
plastic ocean of red—commitment
to proud death. We want there to be a reason
we can like. We want the dead we know
to count, as we don't count the dead we don't.

Body house

Hazel stands in front of me
and points to her eyes.
They are windows, her ears,
they are windows, and her mouth,
she says it's a door.

Her body is a house,
and she's home
for now.

Acknowledgments

Some of these poems have appeared in *Rhythm Poetry Magazine* (online, 2009), *Rogue Stimulus: The Stephen Harper Holiday Anthology for a Prorogued Parliament* (Mansfield Press, 2010) and *Hardscrabble* magazine (2009).

A giant thank-you to Zane, my closest reader, for love and partnership, and to Hazel and Arthur for keeping me on my toes and ears.

For continued camaraderie and support, I thank Mimi Fautley, Nancy McCarthy, Elisabeth Bailey, Alison Smith, Lance La Rocque, Drew Klassen, Alexa Fotheringham, and Mike O'Neill. Good humour; good food; good conversation!

Gratitude to Stuart Ross and Denis De Klerck of Mansfield Press, for their hard work and encouragement.

Alice Burdick lives in Mahone Bay, Nova Scotia, with her husband and two children. She has also lived in Toronto (where she was born and raised), Espanola, Halifax, Vancouver, and on the Sechelt Peninsula. In the early 1990s, she was co-editor of The Eternal Network, and assistant coordinator of the Toronto Small Press Fair. Her work has appeared in magazines including *Dig, What!, subTerrain, This Magazine,* and *Who Torched Rancho Diablo?* She is the author of many chapbooks and two previous full-length poetry collections, *Simple Master* (Pedlar Press) and *Flutter* (Mansfield Press). Her work has also appeared in *Shift & Switch: New Canadian Poetry* (The Mercury Press), *Surreal Estate: 13 Canadian Poets Under the Influence* (The Mercury Press), *Pissing Ice: An Anthology of 'New' Canadian Poets* (BookThug), *My Lump in the Bed: Love Poems for George W. Bush* (Proper Tales Press), and *Rogue Stimulus: The Stephen Harper Holiday Anthology for a Prorogued Parliament* (Mansfield Press).

Other Books From Mansfield Press

Poetry
Nelson Ball, *In This Thin Rain*
Stephen Brockwell & Stuart Ross, eds., *Rogue Stimulus: The Stephen Harper Holiday Anthology for a Prorogued Parliament*
Gary Michael Dault, *The Milk of Birds*
Pier Giorgio Di Cicco, *Early Works*
Christopher Doda, *Aesthetics Lesson*
Rishma Dunlop, *Lover Through Departure: New and Selected Poems*
Jaime Forsythe, *Sympathy Loophole*
Jason Heroux, *Emergency Hallelujah*
David W. McFadden, *What's the Score?*
Leigh Nash, *Goodbye, Ukulele*
Lillian Necakov, *Hooligans*
Peter Norman, *At the Gates of the Theme Park*
Natasha Nuhanovic, *Stray Dog Embassy*
Catherine Owen & Joe Rosenblatt, with Karen Moe, *Dog*
Jim Smith, *Back Off, Assassin! New & Selected Poems*
Robert Earl Stewart, *Campfire Radio Rhapsody*
Carey Toane, *The Crystal Palace*
Priscila Uppal, *Winter Sport: Poems*
Steve Venright, *Floors of Enduring Beauty*

Fiction
Marianne Apostolides, *The Lucky Child*
Kent Nussey, *A Love Supreme*
Marko Sijan, *Mongrel*
Tom Walmsley, *Dog Eat Rat*

Non-Fiction
George Bowering, *How I Wrote Certain of My Books*
Pier Giorgio Di Cicco, *Municipal Mind*
Amy Lavender Harris, *Imagining Toronto*

For a complete list of Mansfield Press titles, please visit mansfieldpress.net